TRAINING
ATHLETES
BEYOND
THE
GAME

WRITTEN BY
KENNY SIMPSON

Dedication

When I work on writing books, I generally can put them together pretty quickly, but this book is special to me. Not only does it contain stories of those I have been blessed to coach over the years, but it was also edited and looked over by many that I love. With all that being said, I know there is not one person who has impacted me more than Jamey, my wife. I understood at an early age that I needed a partner that would cause me to strive to live the way God wanted me to live, even when I didn't want to do that. With that in mind, I searched for a woman that would make me a better person, and I found her in Jamey.

"Coach Simpson has a proven track record of coaching success in two states. I've watched him continue to grow and flourish as a head coach through the years."

Eric Cohu, Head Football Coach Little Rock Christian Academy, 5A State Champions (2018) and Former Head Football Coach at Madison Academy, Alabama

"Coach Simpson coached my two daughters at Alabama Christian Academy. Kenny had a positive, lasting impact on both my daughters. He has spent a career encouraging student athletes to be the best they can be not only on the fields of play, but most importantly in life. Kenny is a great husband, father and coach in that order."

Brent Barker, Athletic Director Eagle Mountain Saginaw ISD and Former Athletic Director at Faulkner University

"Kenny Simpson is a leader when it comes to coaching beyond the field of play. He truly lives out the idea that coaching is a calling and a profession of love. Kenny lives out what he has written in this book. He exemplifies the common saying of Faith, Family, and Football. Kenny is a true servant leader—others >self!"

Stewart Hardy, President/Podcast Host of *All In Sports Outreach*

"In a day and age when way too much focus is put on the product, it's good to know that there are still coaches who focus on the process of empowering people!"

Kurt Hines, Head Football Coach Coronado High School

"No man has been prouder of a son than I am of Kenny in all aspects of life - as a son, husband, father, coach, friend, and deacon at the congregation where he worships. All these roles have shaped him into an excellent coach, but most of all his role as a faithful disciple of Jesus Christ. He provides his children, players and students a lasting example of what a Christian should look like, not only by what he says, but how he lives his life."

Lt. Colonel Jeff Simpson, father

"Kenny Simpson is one of the most innovative coaches I have ever met. His ability to connect with his coaches and players at a personal level translates to the football field and gives his teams a competitive advantage. Coach Simpson is a true game changer in life and in football."

Eric Akin, Area Director, Fellowship of Christian Athletes

TABLE OF CONTENTS

Training the Mind 113

Acknowledgments

When you accomplish pretty much anything in life, it is due to the great support system that is set up. No man is an island, and I am definitely a product of those around me.

There are several ladies in my life that have had a huge impact and this book is not an exception. My mother is possibly the most encouraging lady I've ever known, and she has always pushed me to follow my dreams. My mother-in-law is one of the biggest supporters I've known, and she spent countless hours editing this and all my books. Last, but certainly not least is my wife, Jamey, who is truly the "better half" in our relationship. Without her, I would more than likely have taken a bad path. I am forever grateful.

In addition to the ladies that have had an impact on my life, I've been blessed with a father that provided for our family. Many young men don't have the blessing of knowing their dad, and I am probably closer with my father now than before. I have also been blessed with three brothers and a sister who have been very supportive of me. One of my proudest moments was getting to coach with a brother (Thomas) and to coach my youngest brother (Kirk). As a young coach, I did not fully appreciate how great an experience that was.

Military men go underappreciated in our country, and I am very proud of my father, father-in-law, grandfather, and brother, Tom, and their service to our country. All of these men make me very proud. Men like this give people like me the many freedoms I enjoy.

I have also been very blessed because of some great head coaches that took a young coach who already had all the answers and slowly taught him that he didn't even know what he didn't know. Since becoming a head coach I have started to appreciate them even more. Thank you, Matt Clouser and Gregg Baker for giving me the opportunity.

Thank you to the Southside School District for having the faith in me to come in and lead our football program, and sticking with me through some rough rebuilding seasons. Finding people that are loyal to a football coach is rare, and I am forever grateful to Roger Rich, Roger Ried, George Sitkowski, and Dion Stevens for their leadership at our school.

To my former players, I have loved every season I've been blessed to coach. From junior high basketball at Madison Academy, to track and football at Alabama Christian Academy, to football and track at Southside, the impact my athletes have had on me is something I will forever be grateful for. While I have included some stories in this book, I could easily have brought up the memories that I still can recall vividly. As we say at Southside, "Once a Southerner, always a Southerner." That statement goes for all my former and current athletes.

I have been blessed to have worked with some of the best assistant coaches one can have. Many of them are now either leading their own programs or soon will be. A head coach must have a great staff if he/she is going to have any chance to be successful, and I have been blessed to work with some great men of character. I can be difficult to work with at times, but these assistant coaches are some of the best men I've been around.

Forward

I was a basketball player. At least that's what I thought of myself. As I walked the halls of my high school, I was content with that being my identity. I had little to no interest in doing much of anything else. During those high school years, there was a change of the head football coach at our school. The young defensive coordinator would be taking over the program. Many of the current football players were excited to hear about this young man taking over. Not too long after the announcement, that young first year head football coach found me in the hallways of our school. He wanted me to come out and play football for him. I kindly told him that I was a basketball player and tried to move on. That was until that same young new head football coach found me at a school event after hours and asked me to play football for him. My answer was the same. I didn't like getting out of my comfort zone and football would definitely be outside of that. This process continued until he told me to just come and try it out, no pressure, no assumptions, just try.

In life we have several "watershed" moments. These moments are often decisions or situations that will send our life's path in one direction or another. Little did I know that my first day playing football (for this young and new head football coach) would be exactly one of those moments. Coach Simpson was a man of his word. I came out to spring practice and participated and at no point did he pressure or try to coerce me any further. He didn't need to. I remember that first day and falling in love with the game almost immediately. This basketball player ended up settling in at quarterback and fell in love with playing the game. It has been a long time since that spring. There are plays and moments that I remember from my time playing and a lot of moments that I don't. I can tell you that I do remember the atmosphere that was created in that locker room and growing closer with other young men that I hadn't spent much time with before. Most importantly however, I remember the growth that occurred in me as a young man and Christian throughout my time as one of Coach Simpson's athletes.

Some might say, "That seems a little dramatic to say a decision about high school football changed your life." Normally, I would probably agree with you. However, I was the high school student who had no idea what he wanted to do after graduation came. The options for college, major, and career seemed endless and narrowing things down felt impossible. That was until that same young football coach asked me if I would consider helping coach with him. As a young man who didn't have a clue, the possibility to be around the sport and around Coach Simpson was appealing to the point that I agreed. I was immediately bitten by the coaching bug. Coaching helped lead to education. Education led to administration. This past season I was able to help coach our school's football team that played in the state championship game. I have been fortunate to coach state championship winning track teams. I am now able to work as a High School Principal in an incredible school with awesome teachers and students! None of that happens without high school football. That doesn't happen without Coach Simpson. I definitely enjoyed the football. However, it was the personal growth that I experienced through the process that really changed me. It was Coach Simpson's personal investment in me and the rest of our athletes that made the difference.

As a coach/teacher/school leader now, I can see that there is nothing more important than the social, mental, emotional, and spiritual growth of our young people. It is clear to see that students today are growing up in a very different world than we did even just a few years ago. In a world that will strive to pull them in a thousand different directions, it is important for us to take the opportunity to help them find their bearings before their journey gets going too far. Coaching and other leadership positions carry a significant amount of importance and responsibility as it pertains to these preparations. As I ask my students at school who are some of the men and women who have had the largest impact on them thus far, their answers usually include these types of men and women. If I had to guess, you were probably impacted and led to your current position by a man or woman in one of these positions that took the time and effort to help you grow.

In this book, Coach uses personal examples, quotes, scripture and more to illustrate how important it is to coach in a way that will develop your student athletes beyond their physical abilities. I know from personal experience that Coach Simpson is a man who practices what he preaches. I have been the recipient of many of his thoughts and lessons as a player. But I was also blessed to be able to work along-side him and try to help in any way that I could as an assistant coach. Even to this day, I know that if I have any needs or questions that I can call on Coach Simpson for help. Coach's broad and easy approach to this book ensures that readers will receive some helpful insight, challenge themselves as a reader/leader, and provoke thinking on ways to improve. Through these methods, I know that you will be better equipped to handle the responsibility of leading young people through the trials of a season and more importantly the trials of life.

It is my hope that after reading this book you will commit to making a difference in the lives of the students or young people you work with. It is my prayer that you will be able to consistently gauge what is truly important in your programs and practices. Regardless of what role you serve in or the location or demographics of the individuals and students you work with, we all need to strive to develop people "beyond the game".

Clint Mitchell
Offensive Coordinator
High School Principal
Mobile Christian School

Introduction

"Here is a trustworthy saying that deserves full acceptance: Christ Jesus came into the world to save sinners--of whom I am the worst."   1 Timothy 1:15

"Winning is not a sometime thing: it's an all-time thing. You don't win once in a while, you don't do things right once in a while, you do them right all the time." **Vince Lombardi**

I want to start this book off by sharing that there is a very good chance I am one of the most competitive people on this planet. Whether it is football in a winner-take-all game, dominoes with my in-laws, or even *Uno* with my 7-year old, I want to win and often will become a different person because of my desire to win. Competitiveness is more than likely what drove most of us towards coaching. The chance to go out and try to lead your team to victory over another team is an exhilarating experience. And losing a game as a coach is a very miserable experience. I still have to remind myself to breath before talking after a loss.

I also want to say as Paul did in 1 Timothy 1:15: *"Here is a trustworthy saying that deserves full acceptance: Christ Jesus came into the world to save sinners--of whom I am the worst."* I have many stories where I did not live up to some of the ideals of this book. However, I felt these principles need to be taught to the coaches that are working in the mission field of athletics. Mentoring young athletes is a mission field and coaches have the ability to lead in a very unique way. No coach is worthy to represent Christ, but we are all called to do so to the best of our abilities. As I have aged in this profession and gained more perspective, I have understood more and more the impact of a coach, good or bad.

When we realize we are forgiven sinners that needed to be saved, it changes our perspective on everything. To me it helped me to see my athletes as those who need forgiveness and someone to help them, like I was helped. While we must maintain a disciplined team, we also must realize our goal is to reach as many as possible and share the love of Christ with them.

Vince Lombardi famously once said, "*If it doesn't matter who wins and loses, then why do they keep score?*" Clearly one of our goals as a coach is to make our team better each day, and to ultimately have the opportunity to win the games they will play. That is not debatable for those in our profession. Ultimately our job as coaches we will be judged by and sometimes fired for, is to "win" on a scoreboard. So when I make the statement that the scoreboard does not matter, it is because in comparison to all the other parts of coaching high school sports, it needs to be very low on the priority list. We all strive for greatness in our sport on the field or court. But, this book will be more about coaching for a deeper purpose. When it becomes more than that to you, I feel we become what we are meant to be: mentors to the upcoming generation.

Continuing on with Vince Lombardi, he also said, "*Winning is not a sometime thing: it's an all-time thing. You don't win once in a while, you don't do things right once in a while, you do them right all the time*". Simply, winning on the scoreboard can hide many flaws in a program. As a coach we must be about more than winning or losing games. The older I have become and the more I have studied the great coaches, I see they don't focus their time simply on getting wins on the field or court. Instead, they focus on all the attributes in their athletes they are trying to discipline, and generally winning follows this. Many times you will hear this referred to as "the process".

I believe that coaching is a calling. If you are not someone who thinks of this profession as more than just a job, please stop doing it. The role is too vital to the next generation. Bear Bryant once said, "*I tell young players who want to be coaches, who think they can put up with all the headaches and heartaches, can you live without it? If you can live without it, don't get in it*". I love getting to coach every day, but I would highly suggest anyone that is not fully invested needs to look at other professions. Coaching will emotionally, mentally and physically drain you and you must have a strong desire for it to last as a coach.

As you read through this book, think about all the areas which you should be training your athletes. As a coach, I've failed time and time again, by coaching some great fundamental football teams, but I haven't "had time" for coaching them in the areas that will really matter. Coaching athletes should be like raising your own children. If you don't focus on the areas that matter most, you are simply wasting your time. Through this book I will focus on the following areas – *Character, Heart and Mind,* as well as other important areas and items we should be striving to work on with our athletes.

Each chapter will include discussion questions for you to work through. It will also include a few ideas for you to implement in your program. These are simply suggestions, but they may help your program.

My goal in this book is to help gain perspective in the coaching profession. I plan to use the stories of some of the greatest young men (and a few older men) I have been privileged to witness. I am simply a messenger and a very imperfect one at that. My hope is the message rings clearly to each of you in your coaching journey.

Reach out to me if there is any way I can help you in this journey. As I have learned, often the hard way, having a mentor provides so much value.

Kenny Simpson
@FBCoachSimpson
FBCoachSimpson.com
334-549-9382

Part 1

Training the Character

Character comes from the Greek meaning 'to engrave.'

Chapter 1

Why Do You Coach?

"Everyone who competes in the games goes into strict training. They do it to get a crown that will not last, but we do it to get a crown that will last forever."
1 Corinthians 9:25

"*A good coach can change a game. A great coach can change a life.*" John Wooden

If you have decided to become a coach, more than likely you have been influenced through your own time as an athlete. Think back to which coaches you felt made you a better person. Those people are more than likely what made you want to coach. My bet is if you think about these people you can't remember how great they were with X's and O's, but you think of how they manage people. Coaching is a "people" business. If you have become a coach, you must be able to manage people. Because I care for my players, I give them the best chance to compete, but it must be in that order. Many times it becomes about caring for players IF they give you the chance to compete. The love of a coach, like a parent, should never be conditional.

The word "coach" carries a lot of pride for many. It should be a word that represents a great relationship. I am still called "coach" by many in the community, some of them I've never coached, and by former players (many who aren't that young anymore). Those who have chosen this profession understand that it is not an easy profession, but it is a great profession. I fully believe that a true "coach" commits to being a coach for a lifetime, not just a season.

A Coach's Influence

This picture could be the entire section. The power of a coach's influence is more than we are aware if we choose to make it that way. I feel if you are a head coach, God has given you a platform to teach young athletes much more than the sport you coach. I tell our athletes all the time that if they leave our program and all they have learned is how to play football, then we have failed them. I am as competitive as can be, and I'd say my former players and current ones would say we work as hard, or harder, than anyone we will play. However, I attempt to stress to them that I will care for them no matter what the scoreboard says on 10 Friday's each season. As coaches it is imperative that we make sure our athletes know that we love them and will do anything we can to help them become the best person they can be, regardless of the scores during our games.

The word character comes from the Greek meaning 'to engrave'. The main reason we should coach is to help athletes build character. Athletes should learn many traits that we hold as very high in our value system: Perseverance, Discipline, Toughness, etc... Whatever your sport, there will be many opportunities to teach life lessons. When they have learned these skills they will be successful in any occupation they choose. These life lessons are "engraved" on their hearts and in their minds.

Character can be grown and cultivated in all athletes. Some athletes are born with great natural leadership abilities. Some are born with natural athletic ability. Many are born intelligent. The one trait that I think is the hardest to cultivate is having great character. As a coach we must always make this our first priority, over all other skills.

I've shared this story several times before, but I am amazed at some of the "character" shown by my players. One time after probably the biggest "win" in our school's history to that point, I was leaving my office area after everyone had already left...or so I thought. I heard what sounded like someone very upset and another player comforting the player. I wanted to stay out of sight, but also wanted to see what was going on.

Listening in I could hear our starting quarterback, who I thought would be out celebrating, talking to a sophomore defensive lineman. The sophomore was obviously very upset about some very serious issues in his home life, and our Quarterback was telling him about how important he was to him and many other people. I heard scripture being quoted and life advice, and then I heard, *"You know how Coach Simpson says…"* I stayed to finish hearing the conversation and was in awe of the maturity of a 17-year old young man that had his priorities in the right place. I would say this was my biggest "win" of my career. If I wasn't aware of how important "how" we speak to our athletes was before, I became very aware that night.

This young man obviously had some great parents and people involved in his life that taught him to care for others. They taught him what was really important in life. It was great to hear that our staff had been able to contribute in a small way. The impact of coaching goes far beyond the field. If you have been coaching long enough, you have more than likely been impressed with how some athletes seem to have a very high level of character.

Recap

"Everyone who competes in the games goes into strict training. They do it to get a crown that will not last, but we do it to get a crown that will last forever."
1 Corinthians 9:25

Discussion Questions
1. How are you working to "engrave" character in your athletes that will last for a lifetime?

2. Do you have any stories of success where you heard or saw an athlete living a lesson you had taught?

3. How do you work to reach all your athletes and build their character, especially those with a long way to grow?

Application
1. Make a list of qualities you want to instill in your athletes before they leave your program.

2. Write down activities off the field/court to help teach these skills.

3. Come up with a list of people in the community that may be able to help coordinate activities with you.

Chapter 2

Coach Them Like They Are Your Own

"Impress them on your children. Talk about them when you sit at home and when you walk along the road, when you lie down and when you get up."
Deuteronomy 6:7

"A coach is someone who can give correction without resentment."
John Wooden

This is a picture of me during one of my first seasons I was a head coach with my oldest son, Braden. I love this young man more than he will ever imagine, and I will do whatever I can to protect him. Because of that I teach him and work  with him through his success and failure. My job is to make him grow up to be a man of character. I want to push him to be the best he can be, but want him to know that my love for him will not waiver no matter how much he "wins" in sports, grades or love. I will do my best to make sure he understands that I want the best for him at all times, even if that is not what he thinks is the best for him at the time. Being a father does not stop when my son turns 18 and leaves the house, nor does it stop when he makes mistakes in life. There are many times my sons have told me they "hate" me when I am disciplining them, and I tell them what I tell our athletes... *"I love you too much to let you be less than you can be."*

This is a picture of my 18 seniors from the 2019 season and me. As a coach I hope they know the same values I taught my son were also taught to them. We won a lot of games in their career, two conference titles and three consecutive playoff appearances, but their value to me as a coach was not found in wins and losses. If your players know you care for them off the field as a father would care for his son, they understand the firm discipline that comes from your love for them, not simply wanting to win football games.

At the end of each season, which if you qualify for the playoffs is generally not a pleasant one, since only one team can win a state title, we try to give each senior on our team the opportunity to address the team one final time with all of us in the room. As most would guess, this is generally a very emotional time for the players and the coaches, but especially those that are coming to reality that they will never play a game of football again. We did this the first season as kind of a trial run to see how it went, and I cried about as hard as the players did. We have done it every season since.

I want the players to share with those they have led what they want to be remembered most about during their time in our program. Sometimes the players talk about the great experiences, sometimes they talk about being glad to have finished, but almost everyone mentions wishing they could go back and do it all again. I'd highly recommend this for any coach of any sport.

To keep the privacy of my former athletes, I will not tell any names, but here are a few that have stood out to me over the years -

One senior didn't want to stand up. His comments were similar to several others I have heard throughout the years. *"I don't want to take my pads off, because I don't want this to end. I would do anything to go back and play this season over again".* Then he looked at the underclassmen and said, *"Don't take this for granted; I will be back to watch you guys. Be better than our group was".* The pain was raw and real, and it was evident to the entire group how much it meant to him. Watching this young man realize that he wanted our program to continue to grow even though he would not be able to continue to play showed that we had made an impact on him.

Another senior was at peace with how the season ended. He had been a great leader for our team for his three-seasons. His comments have also been echoed throughout the years. *"I have tried to give all I had over* these past seasons, but looking back I wish I had been more mature early on. You guys need to listen to what the coaches here are telling you. They care for you and want what is best for you". Again talk about humbling for our staff to hear. He was at peace, but all of the coaches were emotional to lose him. The message rings true to players when they hear it from leaders on your team.

The final story I will share is one of our seniors around my first season as head coach that said the following, "I want to thank you guys for accepting me on this team. I don't have a great family life, and you guys were like family to me." I am sure in most schools across the country we would hear similar comments from graduating seniors. One of the goals of each program should be to hear that the team was "like family". When you hear statements like this it causes you to want to become an even better role model for your team.

The goal is always to watch players grow, from whatever maturity level you inherit them, into a better place. Stress to your players any chance you get how much you care for them, and how that means you will work to make them the best version of themselves possible. While that may mean difficult times early on, those who know your intentions for them will accept your coaching.

When you coach players like they are part of your family, there will be uncomfortable and challenging times. Those are the times your athletes will grow the most. But you cannot coach them hard if you do not love them more. Showing them the "why" of discipline is the most important part.

Recap

"Impress them on your children. Talk about them when you sit at home and when you walk along the road, when you lie down and when you get up."
Deuteronomy 6:7

Discussion Questions -

1. If you treated each athlete like your own child, would it look different? How so?

2. Kicking athletes off the team is sometimes needed. How will you handle that situation and what will you do to attempt to keep an athlete?

3. What are you doing with your athletes after you are "done" coaching them?

Application

1. Get to know the home life of your athletes. Find out what their relationship is like with their parents/role models.

2. List your athletes who are at "higher risk" than others.

3. Come up with a system for athletes to approach you with needs.

Chapter 3

Working With Families

"My son, keep your father's command and do not forsake your mother's teaching."
Proverbs 6:20

"In every conceivable manner, the family is a link to our past, and a bridge to our future." **Alex Haley**

When we lose sight of what I feel we are called to do, which is mold young athletes into people of character, we are disappointed when the season ends due to a loss. When we have the right mindset as coaches, we are disappointed because we will not have as many opportunities to mentor our senior class as they graduate. As a coach, realize you have a limited time to work with these athletes, but your mark on them will last a lifetime. As I have become an older coach, I am able to continue to work with the young men that were a part of my program as they become husbands and fathers. Coaching does not end when your players graduate. You just have fewer opportunities to teach.

As coaches, looking at an athlete's background will give us a much better idea as to what obstacles they may face. To that end, I do my best to get to know families of my athletes. While we tell our athletes we do not make excuses, we do need to be aware of where the athlete is coming from. One of my goals in our program is to train the next generation of parents, showing and teaching how a father-son, mother-son, father-daughter and mother-daughter relationship should look. Some athletes are coming from a great situation, and some are not. They do not control the situation, but they can control the future.

Our program does a father-son retreat each season, and while we have some great men that are involved in our program, each season we have multiple young men that don't want to attend. We started having assistant coaches fill in for those who had no male father-figure. My assistant coaches that fill this role will forever understand the importance of their relationship with these players. Be sure you are working hard with not only your players, but your assistant coaches on the impact they are leaving on these young men. Due to the nature of being a head coach, I am not able to be as close to every player as I was during my time as an assistant coach, so it is crucial to teach your younger coaches what you expect from them as a role model for the players.

When we realize that often we are serving in the role of the main role model for our athletes, the weight or responsibility hits hard. While we cannot save each athlete, I feel we are called by our creator to sow the seed to the best of our ability. This retreat also helps those who are blessed enough to have a father who loves them as they get to spend much needed time together. The goal of the retreat is for the athletes, but I often find it affects the fathers even more. As a coach we are given a platform to promote relationships within families, and this retreat has become one of the best things we do to promote it.

One of my coaches, and a major reason I became a coach, was Ronnie Peacock. He has started the concept of this retreat and you can find more information on his website: http://www.father-sonlegacy.com/

This picture is of our "trust-walk" from one of our Father-Son Retreats. Each activity is to work as a symbol for parts of the father and son relationship. This specific activity is letting the son take the lead.

The next activity we started was our Mother-Son date night. The goal is to teach young men how to treat ladies, especially their mothers. We have done multiple different activities and have always had a great time. We also teach "how to hug" your mom lessons. The boys collect the mother's food, open the door for them, escort them to the table and do all the things we expect them to do in order to show their respect for their mother. Teaching your athletes how to respect their parents and honor them is something our society needs.

Many mothers are often ignored and not appreciated by athletes through High School. This is an opportunity to teach the importance of respecting and honoring the most important person in many of our athletes' lives - their mothers. While the night is meant to be a fun experience, we are sure to tie in the importance of the relationship between a mother and son. Often I have my seniors write or read something to their mothers showing their love for them.

These are some pictures of our Mother-Son date night in 2019. Activities we have used include paint parties, movie nights, pizza parties and more. The goal is to get players and their mothers to interact in a relaxed environment.

Remember that no matter what relationship these young athletes have with their own parents, that one day they will be the next generation of parents. Teach your athletes the way parenting should look, and work to mend the bonds between parent and child if possible. The family is a broken institution in our society. Working to repair relationships, or teach how to overcome is a difficult job to say the least. But if we want to truly impact our athletes, it is a job that we need to address.

Recap

"My son, keep your father's command and do not forsake your mother's teaching." **Proverbs 6:20**

Discussion Questions

1. How do you work with your athletes and their families?

2. What are some things you can do to teach how to be a good father/mother to your athletes?

3. How do you work with those in your program that don't have a great relationship with their family?

Application

1. Work to set up an activity to involve parents in your program. I'd recommend a fun simple interactive activity.

2. Identify those athletes in your program that may have a rough home life.

3. Pray for and find ways to mentor all your athletes in their future role as parents.

Chapter 4

Priorities

"Train a child in the way he should go, and when he is old he will not turn from it". Proverbs 22:6

"Your decisions reveal your priorities".
Jeff Van Gundy

In an increasingly diverse world, opportunities to learn how to work together with a wide range of people who start out on equal footing should not be lightly dismissed. The football field, volleyball court, track, basketball court or baseball field do not care about your race, socioeconomic level or IQ. They are the ultimate equal playing fields and there are very few places left that we can teach so many different backgrounds that come together for a common purpose.

Our goal as coaches is to make sure that we take the lessons we can teach through sports and make them into life lessons. While these principles will help in the now and your current team, more importantly they will carry on into the lives of these young men as they become husbands, fathers or wives and mothers. These lessons will continue to serve the players you coach well, long after you have worked with them.

Many times during my career, I have seen a team that is one of the best that we have faced with X's and O's not win many games. Getting your team to play with phenomenal effort should be goal number one for any coach when discussing their play on the field or court. Teaching the fundamentals of the game is important, but when your players are playing for something greater than themselves, they will play harder than the opponent. While scheme is important for coaches to understand and fundamentals are as well, the coach who can reach the heart of his athletes always has the best chance of being successful on and off the field.

Try to remember that discipline is not something you do to punish your athletes. If you love those you are coaching it is actually something you are doing to help them. I have often told my athletes and children that, "I love you too much to watch you give less than your best."

Priorities

I have used visual illustrations in the past to bring home a larger point. One of my favorite ones that I am sure I took from someone else was this one:

I brought in two 50-gallon fish tanks, and beside each tank I placed the following items: 10 pounds of sand, 20-25 small rocks, 10-12 large rocks and 1 very large rock (about ½ the size of the entire fish tank). I told the audience (this was a church event), that each fish tank represented our lives. Each item would represent our values and time spent:

The sand was the events we enjoyed doing that had no inherent evil or good. For example, if we enjoyed fishing or hunting. Or they could represent watching movies or collecting different items. These are pretty much our hobbies or "me time". There is nothing wrong with taking time for yourself or having hobbies, as we all have them. It is good to have hobbies and interests, but these are not considered to be "needs".

The small rocks represent our things we feel we need to do that will advance ourselves socially, educationally or professionally. These can be things like: getting our masters' degree, joining the rotary club, or working for an extra organization. Taking our family on vacations or working another job to be able to provide more for our family could also fall into this category. These are very good uses of time, but also not "needs".

The larger rocks represent things we do that are more important to us and are areas in our life that we prioritize. These can include: Church functions, going to work, volunteering for a good cause, or spending time with those we care about. These are usually values we want to make sure we accomplish in life. Most of us would consider these uses of time as areas that are very important.

The final large rock represents our relationship to God. Not just things that surround God, like attending Church or FCA, but an actual relationship with our creator. How much time are we focusing on the most important aspect of who we believe gave us life?

In the first tank as I was explaining what each of these items represent, I filled up the tank at the bottom with the sand. As soon as it was dumped in the tank it was already half-full. The next items I took were the smaller rocks and I explained that this was where most of us spend a lot of our free time. Now the tank was almost full, but there was a little room left. I then asked the audience what we should put in next, our family time or work. Obviously, they didn't want to choose, so I attempted to fit as many larger rocks in the tank as possible until it was over-flowing. There was not enough room to fit the largest rock as we had already filled our time with everything else.

Then I filled up the next tank. In the second tank I explained we would try things a little differently, and prioritize our time. Once I put the largest rock into the tank it was half-full, but something strange happened. After placing all the large rocks in, I still had room. Then after placing all the smaller rocks there was very little room. The part that surprises everyone is that the entire bag of sand will trickle down and fill the tank, but not overfill it.

The obvious application is that we must be sure to PRIORITIZE our time, and it is amazing what will get done. With your athletes be sure to prioritize what is most important, and it is certainly not scheme or X's and O's. The same is true with your assistant coaches. Be sure to spend time on the heart of your athletes and all the other items you want to accomplish seem to fall into place. Instead of "fitting in" time to train the character of athletes, it should be the center of what we do. And just like the tank illustration, the irony is that when God is at the center of our lives, most other things just seem to fit.

There are many great programs that can help with organizing and setting up times to build character, but the reality is this is best done in an individual manner.

As a coach, you must invest the time to know their character strengths and weaknesses and address those. We spend countless hours identifying the strengths/weaknesses as players, but often neglect the most important area. It always comes down to what we prioritize in our program.

Recap

"Train a child in the way he should go, and when he is old he will not turn from it". **Proverbs 22:6**

Discussion Questions

1. If you asked your athletes what your priority list is, what would they say?

2. What is one thing you hope your athletes take from their time with you?

3. Do you have a personal goal list? What is on it?

Application

1. Write down your athletes and list their strengths/weaknesses. Get help from assistant coaches if needed.

2. Set a time to meet with each athlete 1-on-1 to talk about their life. Do not use this time to talk about the sport or any "X and O" issues.

3. Continue in prayer for each athlete specifically.

Chapter 5

More Than A Game

"Not only so, but we also glory in our
sufferings, because we know that
suffering produces
perseverance; **4** *perseverance, character;*
and character, hope."
Romans 3:4-5

"You don't know why they happen. But when things like that happen, you grow closer together as a family, as men"
Gregg Baker

As a coach we have the opportunity to teach, but often we have the opportunity to learn. I thought I knew that sometimes sports are more than just a game, and then I had the opportunity to watch one of the best young people I have been able to coach, show me what it really looked like:

My last year as an assistant coach, I had a sophomore starting safety named Jordan Creel. He was 5'10", 145lbs that season and was one of the most physical 145lb players I've ever coached. More important than that, he played the game at 110% at all times. Our team that season was struggling, but Jordan was a bright spot for us. I can't remember very many plays that season that Jordan wasn't on the field for us. With that as the background here is his story:

http://www.southeastsun.com/sports/article_43078a3e-3969-596e-9380-99ee08253649.html

Shortly after Alabama Christian Academy's improbable 24-21 win against Daleville, the Eagles' players hoisted running back Jordan Creel into the air and carried him off the field. It was a fitting tribute to the sophomore. Creel had carried ACA for most of the game. He also carried a heavy heart.

Creel's mother Karen, 43, died in a house fire early Thursday morning.

The Eagles rallied around their teammate. Having won just one game entering Friday's contest, ACA never trailed by more than four points against Daleville. The Eagles took the lead late in the third quarter on a 35-yard touchdown run by Creel. ACA finished the game with a 5-minute drive and three kneels on the Daleville 1-yard line.

"You can't understand why things like that happen," ACA head coach Gregg Baker said. "You don't know why they happen. But when things like that happen, you grow closer together as a family, as men. We've had to. It's hurt everybody.

"For those guys to come out and play the way they did tonight, especially that one wearing No. 1 (Creel), is out of this world."

Creel rushed for 232 yards and two touchdowns on 29 carries. He added nine tackles on defense. His efforts earned Creel the Alabama Sports Writers Association offensive player of the week and the Montgomery Advertiser *Great 8* Player of the Week.

Baker received a phone call from Creel at 3:55 a.m. on Thursday informing him of the tragedy. He immediately went to see Creel.

"He's almost like a son to me," Baker said. "I just told him we were going to get through it and gave him some time on his own."

Baker returned Thursday night and told Creel to let him know what he wanted to do. Creel responded that he "wanted to get back to what he does as soon as he could."

By the time the team bus pulled into Daleville, Creel's mind was set.

"When we got here he said, 'Coach, I'm playing,'" Baker said. "I said, 'Strap it on and let's go.' He played for his momma."

"That wasn't a question," Creel said of his decision to play. "(Baker) told me to do what I wanted to do. It *wasn't a question. I knew she would want me to be out here, want me to carry on my routine."*

Daleville head coach Sam Holland spoke to the ACA team after the game, telling them he would keep Creel and the ACA program in his prayers.

"Here's a young man who lost his mother on Thursday and comes out and plays like that," Holland said.

"That's a tribute to what high school football is all about. My heart goes out to him and his family."

Jordan's story was also picked up by Sports Illustrated:

https://www.si.com/high-school/2007/10/31/jordan-creel

"I didn't know what to say," says Creel. "There was a lot of crying, and I think I gave every person in the stands a big hug."

The tears weren't just for Creel. They were also for his mother, Karen, a 43-year-old mother of three, who died of smoke inhalation the night before when the family's home caught on fire.

Creel didn't decide until about half an hour before the buses were leaving from the high school parking lot, when after much back and forth he realized that his mother would have wanted him to play. Creel did show up, his No. 1 jersey in hand, holding the football bag that on any other Friday afternoon would have been packed by Karen the night before. His teammates greeted him with a round of applause. Then, not knowing exactly how to react, they fell back into their usual pattern of telling jokes and playing around.

The tone changed once the team headed into the locker room. There, a somber Baker led the team. "I pulled Jordan aside and said, 'You're going to have the game of your life tonight, and your mama's going to have a front row seat," Baker says.
Creel had some words of his own for his teammates. Once the coaches left the locker room, Creel told his fellow Eagles, "I know she loved me and I know you all loved her, so let's go out there and play for her."

And in the words of Baker, "By golly, they did."

Creel's performance earned him the Alabama player of the week. Somewhere beneath the white lights of Daleville High's football field, Karen Creel's 5-foot-10, 144-pound son played through his grief and rallied those around him to play through theirs. "Every time I touched the ball, I thought of her," Creel says.

There were other signs of remembrance for the woman who every Friday night was "the loudest voice in the stands." The players wore black tape on their jerseys and helmets with Karen's initials written in white-out. Daleville coach Sam Holland, rather than consoling his own team's loss, focused his attention on the Alabama Christian sideline, commending Creel's dedication to his teammates and the memory of his mother. When Holland got word of Karen's death, he called his players out of class to say a prayer for the Creel family. Perhaps that's why the Daleville players were touched by Creel's performance that Friday night, offering their condolences at midfield rather than the customary "good game."

As an assistant coach I was speechless after watching this display of heart on our field. Not just by Jordan, but our team that year had one win in the season and several of the seniors and juniors were already waiting on basketball season to arrive. Not on that night however, they played as hard as I'd ever witnessed. The game became about more than just a game for them. It was about Jordan. It was obviously a night that Jordan showed his character, but it allowed our other players to show that they could do more if they worked for each other.

The best part of this story is not just one night, but that Jordan continued to show great character in all he did. The next season, I would be given my first Head Football position at the age of 27-years old. Jordan would go on to be a 2-time All-State player for our school. He was honored after his senior year by the Montgomery Quarterback Club Player of the Year as well as being our Conference Player of the Year. Due in a very large part to him, our school would turn around a program that had been 4-16 the previous 2-seasons to our first 4A home playoff berth.

Jordan Creel rushed for 1121 and 18 touchdowns this season. During his career at Alabama Christian he rushed for 3421 yards and 35 touchdowns, both school records. Jordan was a two-way starter in 2009, and recorded 45 tackles, 13 pass deflections, and 8 Int's as a defensive back.

Jordan was selected in 2009 and 2007 for the Club's Player of the Week award. He is the first Alabama Christian player to win the award. Jordan also plays baseball at Alabama Christian where he has been an all-state selection the past two seasons.

https://www.wsfa.com/story/11923120/montgomery-qb-club-announces-09-winners/

Jordan's story would continue as he went on to take the lessons learned in high school and become a Doctor. He went through adversity through his entire life, yet he found people that believed in him and showed what can be done if you will persevere.

https://www.montgomeryadvertiser.com/story/sports/college/alabama-state/2018/08/01/whats-up-doc-creels-journey-today-inspiration/873213002/

That's not the end of the story either. Jordan and Coach Baker's relationship stayed strong even when Coach left to take another job. I had the honor getting to be the Head Coach for Jordan's next two season, but Coach Baker was still very much the mentor in Jordan's life from that point on.

Jordan has gone on to do great things with his life. What I'd like to point out is how close Coach Gregg Baker has stayed with Jordan throughout his life. When you become a great coach, you become a mentor for life. During Jordan's time with Coach Baker, they didn't win many games on the field, but during the decade after they've experienced something much greater. When I think of what a coach's impact should be, I think of Gregg Baker.

Recap

"Not only so, but we also glory in our suffering, because we know that suffering produces perseverance; perseverance, character; and character, hope."
Romans 3:4-5

Discussion Questions
1. Have you ever had a player dealing with a situation like Jordan? How did your team respond?

2. Coaching is all about relationships, so what are you doing to build lasting relationships with your players?

3. Have you been able to watch your athletes overcome adversity? How did you help guide them through?

Application
1. If you are able, contact former athletes you have coached and ask if they have any needs you can help fulfill.

2. Ask your players to list a situation they have overcome in their life. Use this as a teaching moment about perseverance.

Part 2

Training the Heart

Humility / Effort / Adaptability / Respect /
Trailblazer

Chapter 6

Training The Heart

"Above all else, guard your heart, for everything you do flows from it."
Proverbs 4:23

"When your legs can't run anymore, run with your heart". - **Unknown**

When we are talking about how to work on the heart of our athletes, here are a few topics we want to be sure to cover. Think of this Acronym for Heart:

Humility

Effort

Adaptability

Respect

Trailblazer

Each of these attributes contributes to what most coaches simply term "H.E.A.R.T". If we can teach our athletes to focus on being humble, or giving great effort, we are not just teaching them a sport. We are teaching their hearts.

In the next chapters I will go in detail over those attributes, but right now I wanted to focus on how we are molding the next generation. The platform given to those who have the honor of the name "coach" is huge. Many times these athletes look to us and respect our words more than any other mentor they may have in their life, even their parents. If you do not feel the pressure of the responsibility towards your athletes, I'd highly recommend you re-think why you are coaching or some of the methods you are using.

As coaches we must guard our heart also. This profession will test and challenge, and at times come very close to break, us. Many times the qualities we are trying to teach our athletes, we must continually develop. It can be easy as a coach, or even a parent, to succumb to the temptations of anger toward a player. Showing HEART for me is all about doing what is right even when it would be easier to do something else.

One of my favorite sports to coach is track and field. In my opinion this sport quickly teaches HEART. When thinking of good examples of this I quickly thought of two young ladies I had the privilege of coaching.

The first was Ashton Foss. She decided to pick up track early in her career and picked, in my opinion, one of the hardest events, the 400-meter dash. I can vividly remember her running in each meet and then going over to help her as she would run to the point of sickness, every single time. My wife was our girls head track coach. Each time Ashton would get up to run she would cheer her on and then go help her attempt to recover. To run to the point of sickness is one of the character traits I point out with my own children of showing heart.

Ashton was unique because of the way she practiced. When timing her practice runs, which every athlete hates, we noticed she would struggle to finish practice and often get sick. When we investigated it further we realized she was running the same times in practice that she was at the meet. She was pouring her heart out every day.

The next young lady is Lacey Smith. Lacey decided to give athletics a chance in the 9th grade. Track was her first competitive sport she would try. With her natural ability, we felt she would be very talented, and we were right. What we did not count on was her severe asthma. Each time she would push herself she had to find the courage (heart) to face her fear. Lacey went on to have a very successful career in our track program, but what I remember most was how impressed I was that she pushed on even in the face of her fear.

While I am very proud of both of these young ladies' accomplishments (both placed at the state track meet in multiple years) I am more proud of the heart they showed during their times as athletes. The goal for me as a coach was to help them push through their fears/limitations with support. To me the definition of heart is pushing through when every part of you wants to quit.

As a coach, often my biggest mistakes are to focus too much on simply teaching my game and not focusing on the larger picture of molding young athletes. Many times we lose the forest for the trees as coaches, or get caught up with things that are temporary and never "get around" to working on the larger issues of teaching life lessons to our athletes. Be very intentional to schedule time to mold the hearts of your athletes. This can be done in many ways: book studies, guest speakers, etc... However, in my experience the lessons that stick best are those that happen because a coach is looking for the right timing and seizes the opportunity when it presents itself. This can only happen if a coach is living the lessons they want to pass on to their athletes.

Programs and resources are wonderful, but the only way to be truly effective is on an individual basis. Look for the opportunities. As coaches we have a "captive audience". These young men and women come to us by choice each day. Be sure to focus on the H.E.A.R.T.

Recap

"Above all else, guard your heart, for everything you do flows from it."
Proverbs 4:23

Discussion Questions

1. What are you doing as a coach to "guard your heart"?

2. How are you incorporating character building in your program?

3. How are you looking for opportunities to reach individual athletes?

Application

1. Make a list of ways you can continue to develop the H.E.A.R.T. of your athletes.

2. As the Bible says, pray for those who persecute you. Now put it in practice and make a list of people that you are having a hard time with (players, parents, administrators), and pray for them. Ask God for guidance in dealing with them and any issues you may be facing.

Chapter 7

Humility

"He has shown you, O mortal, what is good. And what does the Lord require of you? To act justly love mercy and walk humbly with your God". Micah 6:8

"Humility does not mean you think less of yourself. It means you think of yourself less". **Ken Blanchard**

In my opinion, football is inherently the easiest sport to coach when attempting to teach working together as a team. In baseball, coaches can win with a dominant pitcher. In basketball, one great player can carry a team. However, in football, it is very hard for one guy to win games by himself. The offensive line position in football may be the most selfless position in all of sports. This is a position where the entire job is to help others succeed. Those who coach other sports must work even harder to create humble athletes that work toward a common goal. Find ways to reward those who give great effort, not those born with natural talent. If you coach basketball or another similar sport, you must get the team to buy into sacrificing for each other, which is very much counter-cultural.

"Selfless not selfish" needs to be the message we are pushing in all sports. When we point out the players on our team, we attempt to not point to simple athletic achievements. We want to point out great blocks or great hustle by our players. We also strive to point out when players do great things off the field. This doesn't have to be in an "award" setting, but it does need to be recognized and acknowledged from the coach to the athlete. This message is counter-cultural and must be taught.

We attempt to honor as many athletes as possible that are not the "stars" of the team. From "Scout Team Player of the Week" to "Lineman of the Week", we want to make sure we are honoring those that sacrifice for our team to be great. It sounds ironic that we would want to give an award to those that are working to be humble, but as coaches, we want to show that those who simply come to work without concern about statistics or fame are the players on the team that have great character.

Often as coaches we are having to fight against cultural norms to promote humility. Teaching the team to sacrifice for others to succeed has become much harder to do each season. As a coach, we must not only coach this character trait into our athletes, but we must live it out. In a very "proud" arena (athletics), I have found that many of the most successful coaches are those that have realized humility is a very important trait.

While researching humility, I came across this story:

One hot afternoon on a beach, people noticed a young girl drowning. They quickly rescued her. The little girl was unconscious. An old man from a nearby cottage hurriedly reached for the girl laid down on the seashore. As the old man was about to hold the girl, a furious guy warned the people surrounding the girl to step aside, including the old man.
"I was trained to do CPR. Stay out of this! Let me do it!" the guy exclaimed.

The old man stood up and stepped behind the guy and watched quietly while the latter was performing CPR for the girl.

After almost a minute, the little girl regained consciousness. The people around them felt relieved and began applauding the guy. The old man, who looks very happy, gratefully congratulated the guy as well.

After two hours, however, the guy who saved the girl suddenly felt too much fatigue, experienced difficulty in breathing and became unconscious. A few minutes later, he woke up in an ambulance rushing him to the nearest hospital. Beside him was the old man he saw earlier at the beach now checking his pulse rate. The old man did the CPR on him while he was unconscious. This time he learned that the old man is a doctor.

"Why didn't you tell me you're a doctor?" he asked.

The doctor just smiled and answered: *"It doesn't matter to me whether you call me a doctor or not. A precious life is in danger. I became a doctor, not for fame, but to save lives. We had the same goal, and that was to save the girl. Nothing can surpass the feeling that you have just saved another life. There's a lot of things to be protected other than our ego."*

The teary-eyed man humbly said: *"Well, you have just saved two more lives today."*

https://growteach.wordpress.com/tag/short-story-about-humility/

When I first read this story it struck me. How many times have I as a coach jumped right in and thought I knew all the answers? Honestly, too many times. As a coach, be sure to use all your available resources, and I am not just talking about older coaches or administration. If you are knowledgeable of the Word of God and prayerful, you will be able to consult with the best and most humble teacher of all time. Don't come to God as a last resort, but instead allow Him to lead you at all times.

When we read great stories of how truly humble people are it is amazing. The impact a coach can have on his or her players is tremendous if the focus is on others. The platform given to a coach is a great opportunity to teach servant leadership daily to some very open minds. Be sure to teach humility through actions, and actually teach your athletes how to be humble and lift each other up. This world is full of people that want to criticize young people, but teach them how to build others up.

Work hard to allow your athletes to struggle and learn. They will not always remember what you say to them, but they will remember what you teach them. And most of them learn best when they work through it themselves. My principal often asks if we are teaching or the students are learning. It is not the same thing. Just because I have grasped the concept does not mean the students have learned.

Recap

"He has shown you, O mortal, what is good. And what does the Lord require of you? To act justly love mercy and walk humbly with your God". **Micah 6:8**

Discussion Questions

1. How are you teaching humility to your athletes?

2. In our profession often humility does not mix with career advancement, so what do you personally do to keep yourself in check?

3. What are you doing to allow your athletes to grow, by stepping back and letting them lead?

Application

1. Come up with a list of people to thank for what they have done in your life. Call, text or write them and let them know how grateful you are for what they have done for you.

2. Have your team write thank you notes to those that have helped them in their journey.

Chapter 8

Effort

"Whatever you do, work at it with all of your heart, as working for the Lord, not for human masters." Colossians 3:23

"Effort is only effort when it begins to hurt." **Jose Ortega y Gasset**

If you look very closely at this picture, one of my favorite pictures of all time, you will see that it is 4th and 25. Not a good down for any offense. If you look even closer, you see that we are also under a minute in the game. Also, not a good place to be if you are down 6 points, which we were in this rivalry game. This player is Brent Teel. Brent provided one of the plays I'll never forget.

Our team was down 13-7 at our own 15-yard line on 4th and 25. As the defensive coordinator, I was already walking away from the play when it began to unfold. We had called some version of "all-go" when our quarterback was getting swarmed under and simply threw the ball to our running back with about 90-yards and 11 defenders to beat. While Brent was always a high effort player, he wasn't exactly the fastest player. During this play, we went back and counted off of film that he broke 9 tackles and simply refused to go to the ground several times as he scored a game winning touchdown. I had never seen a play where a player's effort was at such a high level. After he broke for the first down, by spinning past 3 defenders at one time, you could see the effort and belief from the rest of our players begin to strengthen as they were running ahead to block for Brent. He would cap off his 85-yard touchdown by stumbling into the end zone exhausted. What a play!

As coaches we see great feats of effort, but we must work to create a culture where it is expected. Some athletes will naturally be high effort players, but some must be taught how to work hard. It is natural for coaches to get frustrated with low effort players, but often they have simply not been taught about expectations and/or been shown how hard they can actually play. The goal of coaching is the same as the goal of parenting, getting a young man/woman to continually improve.

One of my favorite slogans to teach our team each season is this, "*The difference between a boy and a man is that a boy does what he has to and a man does what he needs to*". We want to show that true maturity is when a young person realizes that they must show great effort in all areas of life, not just the areas they care about. When our athletes start to apply this principle, they instantly begin to become much better in everything they do. Be sure to not only teach effort on the court/field, but teach it in all areas. This also applies to coaches. We want to do the fun part of the job, but there are lots of jobs that come with coaching that are not things we want to do and we must be willing to do them anyway.

Effort is a huge part of being successful, but is rarely praised outside of high school sports. Many athletes are so concerned with failure they will not give great effort. As a coach, our job is to create an environment that allows failure and applauds effort at all costs. One of the things we have attempted to do in our program is to notice those that are achieving above their "ability level".

What I mean by this is, we want our athletes to know that we all are born with a level of ability, but we can "over-achieve" if we are willing to give great effort. I feel that athletes can recognize when a coach is giving great effort. Are we prepared for all situations? Have we done our research on the opponent? Are we experts in our field? **As coaches we show our effort by the time we give to our athletes.**

Remember the Bible verse: Luke 12:48b - "*From everyone who has been given much, much will be demanded; and from the one who has been entrusted with much, much more will be asked*". As a coach I tell those that are more talented that it will often feel I am harder on them than anyone else, and I use this verse to explain why. The goal for great programs is for their most talented players to be the hardest working players. To accomplish this it will require an intentional effort by the coach.

Recap

"Whatever you do, work at it with all of your heart, as working for the Lord, not for human masters." **Colossians 3:23**

Discussion Questions

1. How are you teaching effort?

2. Do you as a coach model effort for your players?

3. Another question I ask myself often is "Are you busy or productive?" Great effort is great, but what are you doing to make sure it is a productive effort?

Application

1. Come up with a reward system that will fit within your system and reward feats of effort.

2. If you have not already done so, organize your time and dedicate some time to working with your athletes off the court/field.

Chapter 9

Adaptability

"**19** Though I am free and belong to no one, I have made myself a slave to everyone, to win as many as possible. **20** To the Jews I became like a Jew, to win the Jews. To those under the law I became like one under the law (though I myself am not under the law), so as to win those under the law. **21** To those not having the law I became like one not having the law (though I am not free from God's law but am under Christ's law), so as to win those not having the law. **22** To the weak I became weak, to win the weak. **I have become all things to all people so that by all possible means I might save some**. **23** I do all this for the sake of the gospel, that I may share in its blessings."
1 Corinthians 9:19-23

"Stick to your vision, but adapt your plan" **Brian Maggi**

I believe the most successful coaches are those that have core beliefs but are able to find many different ways to teach these beliefs. The apostle Paul said it best in the verses above. To win as many as possible he adapted to his crowd. He did not water down his message, but he found ways to reach and influence people. A coach that only knows one way to coach will never be as successful as he can be.

I heard this story at church from a very wise mentor to me. He told of how people from the church were picketing outside a new strip-club that had opened in their small town. While they were there, the ladies that would be working started to show up for their shift at the strip club. The signs read various things. Most of them were condemning the obvious immoral acts that would be performed in a strip club, but one in particular mentioned those who participated in this action would be "going to Hell". As one of the women made her way through the picketers to go to work, she was verbally attacked and insulted by those standing there, including the woman holding the sign who told her where she would be going. When she heard all this, with tears she replied, "I'm already in Hell".

The story struck a chord in my heart. Many people are in terrible situations due to their own making and their own fault. But often they simply want to be shown a better way. We cannot reach people if we are too quick to condemn those who need our help the most. How often do we hear about how "this generation" struggles with this or that? It is much easier to simply stand off to the side and condemn, than to jump in to help. When coaches choose to really mentor athletes, it will get messy.

I wonder as coaches how often we simply cast aside the problem athletes because of how difficult they are to work with. Or, if we worry more about what the perception is that we would "allow" such action from a member of our team. I've been burned many times by holding onto athletes longer than I probably should have. But if our goal in coaching is to mentor every athlete we are blessed enough to coach, we will try to keep them close by. This does not mean sacrificing our morals and beliefs, but instead teaching those who want to be better.

Often I hear of how disciplined a team is when they dismiss an athlete from the team. While that has to occur in some situations, I feel we have failed if we reach the point of dismissing athletes. I cannot influence those I am not around. In my time as a coach, I have had to dismiss players from the team, and I feel those situations were my biggest failures. The goal is always to adapt to become the mentor that can reach as many as possible.

One of my administrators always told us to "preserve the core, stimulate progress" from Jim Collins book. The concept is the same as the apostle Paul is teaching.

We must have a fundamental belief system and core values, but need to be willing to try different methods to reach more people. I am often asked if I am a "players coach" or a "disciplinarian" and my answer has become, "I am what my players need me to be".

Being adaptable also works with our players. We must teach our players to adapt to help our teams and teach each that they have a valuable role. Since I coach football, I will use that sport as another example. I have had many future Quarterbacks that have played another position while they were waiting for their turn. One of my future Quarterbacks was a Receiver, one was a Tight-End and one was even an Offensive Lineman. Each of these players learned they needed to adapt for the greater cause for our team.

We highlighted this example of how each of these players sacrificed their own hopes and adapted for our team. This has helped our cause as many of the future Quarterbacks and leaders of our team could identify with other positions and gain their respect. When athletes feel like they are part of something bigger than themselves and learn to sacrifice, you are truly getting through to them. One of the most difficult things to do is convince an athlete they need to move to a different role than they are accustomed to performing. To do this a coach must do a great job of teaching all the aspects of the H.E.A.R.T. One is willing to adapt if they realize what they are doing is for the greater good, and athletics are a great place to teach this concept.

As a coach we are challenged each season by several different personalities. We must constantly monitor what method of coaching works for each player individually and work to make sure we are coaching as effectively as possible. Working to reach as many players as possible is the goal of coaching.

Recap

"To the weak I became weak, to win the weak. I have become all things to all people so that by all possible means I might save some." **1 Corinthians 9:22**

Discussion Questions

1. What are you doing as a coach to reach as many players as possible?

2. Each athlete is created different, what are you doing to keep the message and goal the same?

3. Has there been a time you have felt at a loss to reach a player? What have you done to be prepared for future situations?

Application

1. Identify the different methods your athletes learn and come up with strategies to reach them.

2. Write down the "core" of your program and how you will preserve this.

Chapter 10

Respect

"12 Now we ask you, brothers and sisters, to acknowledge those who work hard among you, who care for you in the Lord and who admonish you. 13 Hold them in the highest regard in love because of their work. Live in peace with each other."
1 Thessalonians 5:12-13

"Everyone has a need to be valued and respected. Make sure you give others the respect you would like in return."
Anonymous

Teaching respect is one of the staples of great coaching. I've heard it said if we respect God, other people, and ourselves, in that order, we will be on the right path. In a society that often reverses that order, this is an incredibly difficult task. Fortunately, for us the profession we are in gives many opportunities to teach respect.

Respect can be taught from the daily rituals of cleaning up after ourselves to learning to take defeat with grace. Training athletes that they show respect to the program, by being on time, giving great effort, sacrificing personal goals and cheering teammates success is vital. If your program is to teach the core values that young people desperately need, these must be not only preached, but enforced.

"If you want to go fast, go alone. If you want to go far, go together". - African Proverb

One way to teach this principle is to show how in team sports we are better together. While at first athletes will sacrifice only if they see the benefit for themselves, over time it becomes part of the culture of the team to give up personal glory for the team. This is only done if the players have learned that respect begins outward and works inward.   Honoring God and others must come first.

Teaching athletes that it is acceptable to place others first is a very hard task. The only way they can truly learn is to see it modeled every day by their coach. Servant leadership is needed to show the way respect should work.   When we realize authority is not something to lord over people, but instead a platform to serve, respect between the athlete and the coach begins to build.

The next phase of respect turns inward. Not respecting yourself is often right under the surface with many young athletes. They may show it in different ways, some lash out in anger, some want to quit and others blame everybody but themselves. This is often because they lack security and do not truly respect themselves.

Many times athletes feel they only have value for what they can do. If they were to "fail", they lose their value. Imagine thinking your entire self-worth was tied into what you could do. **As coaches, we must make sure our athletes understand that their value lies in who they are, not what they can do.** Once our athletes recognize they are worth more than a game, they will begin to respect themselves more.

The opposite of this also can happen.   Athletes will think they "respect" themselves, but are actually only full of pride.   Respecting yourself includes the self-awareness to see flaws and acknowledge them, but continually strive to better yourself. True respect for oneself is due to understanding where the value lies. Athletes must be taught that their value is more than a game.

Another area we must address as coaches is teaching athletes to respect their opponents. How many times have we seen on YouTube, or some other form of social media, a post where an athlete belittles their opponent? Many times these videos are shown and praised by everyone. As coaches, we must teach that we respect even those who oppose us in our sport. This is very difficult in an era that is all about winning and image. Teaching respect for our opponents allows us to teach that while we compete for a victory on the field/court, we can carry ourselves with dignity throughout the process.

Coaches must have a healthy respect for themselves as well. Knowing they matter more than what they can do on a court/field should fill coaches with respect for themselves. This is not pride or arrogance. It is simply understanding that our role is to point everyone to the cross. While winning is important for all coaches, it should not be where we place our identity.

Coaches must also work hard to respect those in their field. One of the most difficult parts of this for me is still my relationship with the officials. I struggle in every game to keep a healthy relationship with those who are being paid to officiate the game. It is very difficult to maintain composure when we are naturally competitive people and the intensity can become very high on game day. That is no excuse to take out frustrations on those we expect our athletes to respect.

Finally, coaches must also respect opposing coaches. This profession is a very difficult one already without fighting or lack of respect between competitors. Working with other coaches to help foster respect among the coaching community has become better as the years have passed. Personally, I have been able to witness the coaching community rally to support each other many times. This is one of the best lessons we can teach our athletes. Respect needs to be bigger than a game.

Recap

"12 Now we ask you, brothers and sisters, to acknowledge those who work hard among you, who care for you in the Lord and who admonish you. 13 Hold them in the highest regard in love because of their work. Live in peace with each other."
1 Thessalonians 5:12-13

Discussion Questions
1. What athletes do you have that are struggling with respecting themselves? Why do you think that is?

2. How are you modeling servant leadership?

3. Do you struggle more with pride or self-esteem?

Application
1. Set a meeting with a player that you know struggles with self-respect. Tell them how much they mean to you (do not mention the sport).

Chapter 11

Trailblazer

"A good name is more desirable than great riches; to be esteemed is better than silver or gold." Proverbs 22:1

"What you leave behind is not what is engraved in stone monuments, but what is woven into the lives of others".
Pericles

When I got my first job out of college I was very excited to be heading to Madison Academy in Huntsville, Alabama. I didn't really care what position I would be working with. I just wanted the opportunity to work up the chain of coaching. While there, I was able to work for some great coaches, but one coach I really never worked for still inspires me to this day.

George Bennett was the head football coach at the school I took my first coaching position in 2003. It was known that this would be his final season in that role. I didn't know much about everything that was behind this decision, and still don't really understand it. I just knew that that season I would be coaching junior high football and that there would be a change with the senior high position at the end of that season.

As the season unfolded I watched from a small distance as Coach Bennett was nothing but professional through what must have been a difficult situation. He was hard working, compassionate and inspirational for a 23-year old coach who had no idea how the coaching world worked. Coach Bennett would finish out his last season, making the playoffs, and then be replaced.

I stayed on for two more seasons at that school, eventually working my way onto the varsity staff and was fortunate enough to be part of a great team in 2005. It wasn't until I was a head coach and went through a pretty similar situation that I could truly appreciate Coach Bennett. Caring for your athletes when feeling that everyone around you has done you wrong or may be whispering in the background was a very difficult situation. During the times I wanted to fight for what I believed to be right, I thought back to how George Bennett handled himself. He always put his athletes first, even at his own expense. I knew I wanted to be a George Bennett. I have been blessed since that season to move to a much better situation and in 2012 had my 2nd son. His name...Bennett Simpson.

As coaches we have more eyes on us than we are ever aware. How we react to difficult situations often sets the tone for how your entire program will respond, or even how future coaches, husbands/wives, leaders in our community will respond down the road when they experience difficulty.

I've been blessed to work in some great situations during my time as a coach, but as I have learned there will come challenges. How we shine our light in the darkest situations is who we truly are. I learned that lesson from Coach Bennett and have always tried to remember that my goal is to be the same person through the ups and the downs in our profession.

Recap

"A good name is more desirable than great riches; to be esteemed is better than silver or gold." **Proverbs 22:1**

Discussion Questions

1. Have you ever been through a difficult season? What did you do to handle it?

2. Do you have a mentor or a person you can confide in for difficult moments?

3. Coaches must have thick skin. What are you doing to prepare for the difficult times that you may face?

Application

1. Find a mentor coach. Someone that you do not work for, but can help guide you through difficult times.

Part 3

Training the Mind

G.R.I.T.

Chapter 12

Training The Mind

"Set your minds on things above, not on earthly things." Colossians 3:2

"Coaches who can outline plays on a blackboard are a dime a dozen. The ones who win get inside their players and motivate." **Vince Lombardi**

Almost as important as the heart of your athletes is the mindset of your program. We all strive to be great at football and to learn the game and the nuances of what helps us to be successful on the field. In my opinion, what separates those who will last in our profession is the amount of actual G.R.I.T. they possess.

When examining almost any successful person the quality that seems to stand above all others is G.R.I.T. Talent will take you only so far in our world. Intelligence obviously can help also. Coming from a good situation and having a great support system is also a huge advantage. But the last three traits are "uncontrollable" for us. We must make daily decisions about how much G.R.I.T. we will possess.

As a coach, I am very hopeful each season we will have very naturally gritty kids. But often this is a skill that must be taught to 90% of your athletes. Some are more naturally hard working, and some have farther to go, to put it nicely. Our goal as a coach is to move athletes farther along in this skill. If they have little, the goal is to teach them to have some. If they have some, the goal is to move them to more.

When I think of G.R.I.T. - these are the qualities I associate with it:

Growth **mindset** is something that is a must when working with athletes and coaches. Continuous learning must occur as a leader if we are ever going to get our athletes to follow in our footsteps. I have heard a wise principal once say during a meeting, *"Have you taught for 31-years, or have you taught for 1-year, 31 times"*. Just because we have experience does not mean we are continuing to improve as a coach. We want to continually strive to improve ourselves as coaches.

This is one of the hardest attributes for those that are naturally gifted. Those whose life has come easy due to their ability will struggle the first time they have to dig deep. This goes for coaches as well. It is easy to think we have arrived when we taste success. Those who last in our profession are continually pushing forward. Growth minded people will always attempt to improve through failure and, more importantly, through success.

Resilient people are always going to be much more mentally tough than the average person. Learning to fail and get back up each time is the definition of what I hope to teach my athletes. I often try to work with my athletes about thinking about what they want their lives to look like in 5 weeks, 5 months, or 5 years. What can they do now, however small, to help that goal.

I've been blessed to be around some great schools that understand that a future story needs not only goals, but a plan of action and a plan for when things don't go as planned. Chinese proverb *"The man who removes a mountain begins by carrying away small stones."* Understand that those who last in this profession are not those that never lose, but those who continue through the losses.

This is a picture of one of the most resilient athletes I was ever blessed to coach. Colby Sutton was a senior when I took the job at Southside Batesville High School in 2011. Colby had never experienced a win at the senior high level. His group had been 0-20 going into their senior season. Not only that, but he had not really had a huge role on either of those previous teams. And to make matters even worse, his new coach (me) didn't really see him having a huge role on the team his senior season. Little did I know that Colby was the type of player that was resilient to his core.

During the season it became more and more evident that Colby was the type of guy who made the plays we needed almost through sheer effort and heart. At 160-pounds and not being the fleetest of foot, he was at a major physical disadvantage most nights. Instead of finding all the excuses he could have gone to he kept coming back for more. One of my favorite nights, and the night I realized Colby was special, was the night he ran the ball 41-times for us, often for not so glorious 3-yard gains, into a ferocious defense. He also played every snap on defense and special teams. When I think of resilient people, I think of players like Colby.

Integrity is doing what is right regardless of who may or may not be watching. Teaching athlete's this skill is very difficult and requires a very strong relationship. The goal here is to teach the WHY in all we do as coaches. Why do we push our athletes to compete to the best of their ability? Why do we teach sacrifice for the team? Why do we want them to always be honest and trustworthy?

Integrity is in my opinion one of the least taught areas in the coaching world. It is hard to measure and takes more time to improve on than any other characteristic. It also at times comes in conflict with some natural instincts we have as competitors. Win at all costs is now being preached at the highest levels. As coaches, I feel we are called to teach our athletes that we will not sacrifice our values for anything we may hope to gain. Compete with all your ability, but never sacrifice who you are.

Tenacity is a trait that is shown time and time again in those who are the best in all areas of life. One of my favorite characters in the Bible is the Apostle Peter. He had many occasions that he said the wrong thing or did the wrong thing in the presence of Jesus, but when all was said and done, Jesus told him, *"And I say also to you, that you are Peter, and on this rock I will build my church; and the gates of hell shall not prevail against it"*. I've always had a special place in my heart for his example since I often fail.

Peter is considered one of the greatest Christians to ever live, but remember this is a guy who literally denied knowing Christ in his hour of need...3 times. What set Peter apart from Judas, among many things, was his tenacity... his willingness to get back on track time after time. Peter was also put in his place by the apostle Paul in the early church, Galatians 2:11-13, later in his ministry. Each time he responded correctly, but repenting and continuing to work harder. No excuses, just renewed effort. When I think of tenacity, that is what I think about.

As a high school player, I played for two different High Schools that had the mascot of the bulldog. One of my favorite animals on the planet is the bulldog because of his tenacity. Winston Churchill once said, *"The nose of the bulldog is slanted backwards so he can continue to breathe without letting go."* Often as a coach we gravitate towards those tenacious athletes who refuse to quit. The goal is to have all our athletes become like the bulldog, refusing to quit.

Recap

"Set your minds on things above, not on earthly things." **Colossians 3:2**

Discussion Questions –
1. What area of the G.R.I.T. acronym do you feel is the most important for long term success as a coach?

2. When have you failed as a coach? How did you respond?

3. Think to a time you were challenged in your integrity? How did you handle that situation?

Application
1. Write a note of encouragement to an athlete that is showing great resiliency.

2. Come up with a list of areas you are wanting to improve. Pick one and start through prayer asking God to show you ways to improve.

Chapter 13

Grit

"**24** Five times I received from the Jews the forty lashes minus one. **25** Three times I was beaten with rods, once I was pelted with stones, three times I was shipwrecked, I spent a night and a day in the open sea, **26** I have been constantly on the move. I have been in danger from rivers, in danger from bandits, in danger from my fellow Jews, in danger from Gentiles; in danger in the city, in danger in the country, in danger at sea; and in danger from false believers."
2 Corinthians 11:24-26

"Grit is choosing to lean in and work on your Art when the world thinks it's already good enough." **Rob Beaudreault**

There are several great examples of grit in the Bible, but one of my favorite examples is the apostle Paul. Not only did he do a complete change of lifestyle once he converted to Christianity, but he lived his life through all sorts of persecution. He was eventually killed for his beliefs. The man would not be deterred. His grit got him through. In my opinion, one can only show true grit when they have a cause that is worthy of it, and Paul's cause was most worthy.

As a coach we are often asked how to get kids to "buy in" to our program. I would suggest that you must have something worth "buying" if you want your athletes to truly want to be invested in your program. If the entire goal of your program is to win games, there is nothing that separates it from other programs. When athletes recognize that a program is using the sport to teach about life, that program becomes one that is desirable for "buy in". Great coaches show their athletes that they care about them for more than what the athlete can give the coach.

When I took my most recent job, I was walking into a situation where the team had lost 23 consecutive games. That meant the seniors on that team had NEVER won a game at the senior high school level. My expectation level for the work ethic of the program was not very high to say the least.

What amazed me was the amount of "grit" this group of seniors had. To stay with something for over two years without having any wins had made them some of the hungriest players I've ever had the pleasure of coaching. Working with their phenomenal work ethic, our staff was able to figure out just enough ways that we had some success that season. They had a true love for each other and for their team. When athletes have a purpose that is higher than just a scoreboard, they will show grit.

Of all the character traits we can help pass on to our athletes, grit is the most important. This trait will serve them throughout their entire lives. Often when talking with my team I mention that we are blessed with talents, but we choose to show grit. Talent is something we don't earn, and grit is a trait we can control. *"Grit is living life like it's a marathon, not a sprint."* - Angela Duckworth

One of my favorite moments ever in coaching was to watch them win our first game that season. The amount of emotion is almost impossible to explain, but I have never forgotten the looks on their faces (or their parents and our administration). We had finally "won", but the reality was they had been winners long before we won a football game. They were winners because they had learned the secret of grit -- NEVER QUIT. Once an athlete learns this skill they will be set for life's challenges.

This is a picture from the moment we broke the losing streak. I don't know if I'll ever be able to experience anything like that night again. Watching young men finally get rewarded for years of hard work was an experience I'll never forget.

As coaches we are called to teach grit in our athletes. That is not a fun lesson and is often difficult to teach depending on the circumstances. Again, I find the athletes that struggle the most with this concept are actually those that are the most naturally talented. Those are the athletes that have found success easy and will struggle the most when things become difficult. Working to create situations that all athletes must push beyond their comfort level is very important.

When looking at why some coaches show more grit than others, I believe we need to look for the motivation. As stated early in this chapter, for us to "buy-in" we must have something we want to buy. Setting our minds on things above will help this happen. The key to living with grit is understanding the goal --- reaching our athletes and sharing God's love for them. When this becomes our priority, we can persevere through all struggles.

Recap

"I have been constantly on the move. I have been in danger from rivers, in danger from bandits, in danger from my fellow Jews, in danger from Gentiles; in danger in the city, in danger in the country, in danger at sea; and in danger from false believers."
2 Corinthians 11:26

Discussion Questions

1. Who was the most "gritty" athlete you coached?

2. How do you work to improve the "grit" of the team you coach?

3. How are you working to teach your athletes through difficult times?

Application

1. Come up with a drill/situation to challenge the grit of your team. Explain the purpose and allow them to fail if needed. Once you have completed the drill/situation discuss with them the reactions and teach them how to work through difficult times.

2. Challenge yourself to do something you have been scared to attempt.

Chapter 14

Training The Process

8*"We are hard pressed on every side, but not crushed; perplexed, but not in despair;* 9*persecuted, but not abandoned; struck down, but not destroyed."*
2 Corinthians 4:8-9

"Men are developed the same way gold is mined. When gold is mined, several tons of dirt must be moved to get an ounce of gold; but one doesn't go into the mine looking for dirt—one goes in looking for the gold." **Andrew Carnegie**

Focusing on the result will often be counter-productive. When you are driven to only focus on winning games, there will be sacrifices along the way. As a younger coach, I made several tries to give my athletes the "best opportunity" to win. It is very easy to justify all decisions we make as a coach, but the reality is we understand what is right and wrong, and it is our duty to teach all our athletes character. The ironic part of this process is that once the focus changes from on the field issues to character building, the wins on the field tend to follow anyway.

Too often in our profession we look for the "next" thing in coaching, or the newest program that has promised to turn around your program quickly. The reality is that the most "successful" teams on the field/court often never even talk about winning and losing games. Instead they focus on what many call "the process".

Irony of focusing on process

"If you focus on results, you will never change. If you focus on change, you will get results" Jack Dixon

I've had some great seasons, and I've had some very rough seasons if you look at the result as wins-losses. The great irony I have found is the years we have been "successful," I haven't written down goals of wins or points or anything related to our season. We have simply focused on doing the best we could and ignoring the result at the end of the games. Those seasons we have won two conference championships and set several school records, but we never talked about it. Instead we spoke about practicing hard or working out with great effort, or even sleeping and eating well to give us the best opportunity to be successful.

When we focus on a goal like winning, we become almost like a drug addict --- chasing the next high --- becoming obsessed with reaching the goal --- sacrificing anything in our path to reach our goal. The most disappointing thing about being completely goal oriented is that even if we reach that goal, the high quickly wears off. I can speak to this because that was me. Winning games or even championships is a huge temptation for me, but I have realized that the wins don't satisfy, but the long term relationships do.

Kobe Bryant had this to say after winning his first NBA Championship. *"I can remember winning the first championship and kind of being like, 'Okay, now what? What happens now?' ... [Teammates] celebrating, waving champagne bottles around ... And outside of that, it was, 'Okay, now what?'"* Can you imagine spending your entire life working towards one goal and then once you reach it, those are your thoughts? Speaking with several coaches who have won championships (and having been a part of one in basketball and two in powerlifting) I can say that if that is the only purpose of your life, you will feel empty even if you are to achieve it.

There is nothing wrong with being a coach that is very driven. I would simply caution you to set the "right goal". Winning will often become a by-product for you if you focus on a much larger, more important goal. My personal goal has been: "to grow my athletes into men/women of character by teaching life lessons through the sport they choose to play". I have found one of life's great ironies has become that we have won more since I've shifted my mindset. I have also been much more satisfied with my own situation when I changed my focus to what I feel coaches are called to do. Focusing on the Character, Heart and Mind of our players ensures we are coaching beyond a game.

Working hard for a win is seen often in our world. Getting motivated to beat someone is a great thrill and as a competitor it drives me. However, once we shift our thinking to larger goals, I have seen how much harder my teams play. They have begun to understand that this game is simply a small portion of who they are. While we want to win and compete on game day, our teams have begun to realize that you must "win" in every area of your life and that will carry over onto the field/court.

This is not a short process or a quick solution. It is a long process, and many will quit the process along the way. Our calling as coaches is to continually push our athletes. My teams have often been surprised by my demeanor after games in which we have "won," and I am not happy, or in games we have "lost," but I seem to be ok with the result. While I want to win as bad as anyone, I'm much more concerned with our athletes fulfilling their potential. We want to compete to the best of our ability. The scoreboard really doesn't matter in our assessment.

Recap

⁸"We are hard pressed on every side, but not crushed; perplexed, but not in despair; ⁹persecuted, but not abandoned; struck down, but not destroyed."
2 Corinthians 4:8-9

Discussion Questions
1. When is a time you have been tempted to take a "shortcut" to get closer to winning a game?

2. What character traits do your athletes need the most work on? What traits do you as a coach need to improve?

3. How do you balance competitive nature, with keeping the process as a priority?

Application
1. Come up with your "process" or mission statement for your team.

Chapter 15

Training The Grind

"Not so with you. Instead, whoever wants to become great among you must be your servant," Matthew 20:26

**"The secret to success is good
leadership, and good leadership is all
about making the lives of your team
members or workers better." Tony
Dungy**

One of the terms that is becoming almost over-used is the term "the grind". This is used often to talk about doing the daily jobs that are needed in our lives today. It has become cool to post to social media everything we are doing as we "grind" to get ready for the season.

At first I rolled my eyes at all these posts and felt we were seeing athletes that were simply begging for attention. And while that may be the case in some scenarios, I have started to really like the message behind "the grind". Many times in our line of work we have athletes and coaches looking for the shortcut to success. I have mentioned one of the quotes I have my athletes repeat often in an earlier chapter, but here it is again. "*The difference between a boy and a man* (or you can put girl and woman), *is that a boy does what he wants to do and a man does what he has to do*." Now I attempt to find opportunities to teach this principle, and "the grind" seems to be a great opportunity.

Doing what you enjoy doing is not a grind. It is simply working on what you love. When "the grind" is brought up, your mind should go to the parts that are not as enjoyable in our job as coaches. Those parts are when coaches begin to separate out, and the true servant leaders show up.

"Servant leadership is all about making the goals clear and then rolling your sleeves up and doing whatever it takes to help people win. In that situation they don't work for you, you work with them." Ken Blanchard

One of the hardest lessons I had to learn as a young coach was that there were a lot of parts to coaching I had never thought about. Painting the field, doing laundry, cutting the grass and more were "not fun" jobs. These must be done, but they are far from glorious jobs. To me this is the coaching version of "the grind". Jobs that no one sees or appreciates, but that must be done for your program to succeed.

If we expect our players to do the jobs that must be done for our program, then we better be sure they see us doing those same jobs. While I often fall short in this

area, my goal as a head coach is to never be "above" any job. I want our program to be about "we did" not "he did". This must stop from the top and work its way down

This is Josh Millikin. When I think of players that truly enjoy "the grind", he comes to my mind. Josh started for me his sophomore year as a skinny 140-pound quarterback. I knew it would be a long season for us as we were going to play a lot of sophomores. He was bruised and beaten each game, but kept fighting. As we moved to his junior season, Josh decided to face "the grind" of the weight room and the track. He spent hours going above and beyond what we asked of him. By the time he was a senior, he was a 205-pound college ready quarterback.

But what makes Josh such a great story is not just his love of the weight room, but his true love of "the grind". He would stay after practice to help clean up the locker room. He would spend time checking in on teammates (even those who did not play much). He would even stay behind often and fill water coolers for the next practice. He truly embraced "the grind", and it paid off for him.

He embodied a servant leader as a 17-year old senior. I was amazed and blessed to watch how he conducted himself. He showed me what a leader can do for a program. We had a rough year his first season, but by his senior season we clinched our first ever playoff berth and our program has never looked back. I credit that to kids like Josh Millikin.

In the first chapter I shared this story. The quarterback...Josh Millikin:

Listening in I could hear our starting quarterback, who I thought would be out celebrating, talking to a sophomore defensive lineman. The sophomore was obviously very upset about some very serious issues in his home life, and our Quarterback was telling him about how important he was to him and many other people. I heard scripture being quoted and life advice, and then I heard, *"You know how Coach Simpson says..."* I stayed to finish hearing the conversation and was in awe of the maturity of a 17-year old young man that had his priorities in the right place. I would say this was my biggest "win" of my career.

Finally, the ultimate leader on earth was Jesus Christ. The story that comes to my mind first when I think of servant leadership is this one:

"12 When he had finished washing their feet, he put on his clothes and returned to his place. "Do you understand what I have done for you?" he asked them. 13 "You call me 'Teacher' and 'Lord,' and rightly so, for that is what I am. 14 Now that I, your Lord and Teacher, have washed your feet, you also should wash one another's feet. 15 I have set you an example that you should do as I have done for you. 16 Very truly I tell you, no servant is greater than his master, nor is a messenger greater than the one who sent him. 17 Now that you know these things, you will be blessed if you do them." John 13:12-17

Recap

"Not so with you. Instead, whoever wants to become great among you must be your servant." **Matthew 20:26**

Discussion Questions

1. What are you learning from your players you are blessed to coach? Good and bad.

2. When you hear "the grind" what do you think about?

3. What are some of the jobs you never knew were included in coaching?

Application

1. Find a job that needs to be done that you have been putting off and do it this week.

2. Talk with your team about what "the grind" really is. Not just doing what they enjoy, but what they don't enjoy.

Chapter 16

Mistakes I've Made

"If anyone, then, knows the good they ought to do and doesn't do it, it is sin for them." James 4:17

"When people ask me now if I miss coaching UCLA basketball games, the national championships, the attention, the trophies, and everything that goes with them, I tell them this: I miss the practices." **John Wooden**

One of the most successful coaches ever was John Wooden, who at one point won 10 National Championships in 12 years at UCLA, and he said that about what he missed the most from coaching. The longer I have been fortunate to coach I have realized that even though the wins-losses on Friday night are what many people see, I enjoy the daily practices and the relationships being built throughout the season much more. Working toward a goal and winning is a good thing to do, but don't miss out on the life lessons being built along the way. I've often lost the forest for the trees, by simply focusing on winning ballgames.

If you coach long enough, you have plenty of stories about what your athletes do after high school. I have been blessed to coach some phenomenal young people that have gone on to great things. You also have plenty of opportunities to talk to your athletes in a way that may change their lives. It is difficult for me to share all the times I've failed by words left unsaid, but here is one of the stories:

Garrett Yeager was one of my favorite athletes to coach. When I took a job at a school that had gone two plus seasons without a win, I knew we needed athletes. So when we had a very talented player transfer to us about a month before the season, I figured this was going to be a great thing for our program. Garrett had been in trouble with some alcohol issues and some other legal issues, but I am all for giving young men a 2nd chance, and so this seemed to be a very natural fit.

Garrett came in that season and was awesome to work with. He showed up every day, worked very hard, was very respectful and was very talented. We did let him know he was on a one-and-done strike policy and he abided by it. Our program was blessed by Garrett, and we were doing well by him, or so I thought. He was staying out of trouble through our season, which was his senior year, and we were having the best season to that point in school history. So it was a win-win, until it wasn't.

Halfway through the school year, after football, I heard several rumors about Garrett reverting back to what was always a problem for him. Since he was no longer a football player, it was much easier to simply let it be "someone else's problem". Garrett and I had been pretty close during the season, but after the season I could sense some drifting from him, and those who had attempted to help him stay out of trouble. After graduation, his problems became worse.

https://www.washingtontimes.com/news/2015/dec/28/couple-honor-sons-memory-at-faith-based-camp-in-ch/

CHARLOTTE, Ark. (AP) - *For the 22 men at John 3:16 who will be getting a memory blanket, it's more than just something to keep them warm. It's a reminder of how their own lives mirror the young man who died earlier this year.*

For the past nine months, Brian and Tanya Yeager have been wrapped up in their grief over the death of their son, Garrett Yeager, who would have turned 22 this month. They can identify with the struggle these men are dealing with while staying at the faith-based camp. This is the first time they've publicly shared his story.
The Batesville Daily Guard reports that Brian and Tanya met while Brian's son Garrett was attending the day care where Tanya was working and would later own.

The two got married, and Tanya said it wasn't easy blending two families into one, but they raised their children by the Word.

Garrett was a good kid, she continued, but around age 14 he started drinking. He was on the football team and that was the "cool" thing to do.

"I can't tell you how many times we were called to come get him. ... It was just about every weekend," Tanya said.

She and Brian helped Garrett get a hardship license and got him a vehicle at 14. "For lack of better words, we gave him the rope he hung himself with."

Garrett struggled first with alcohol, and that led to drugs.

He was smart and played football and baseball; he loved hunting and the outdoors, and he would do anything for his family and friends. So when he began his foray into drugs, he became almost unrecognizable to those closest to him. Tanya and Brian were in disbelief: "Not our kid ... This can't be our life."

It was three years ago this month that something nagged at Tanya in the back of her mind. Garrett was 18 and had moved out, not wanting to abide by their rules, and Tanya just had a feeling urging her to go by and see Garrett. "When your kid is in trouble, you know."

She and Brian were sitting in church when she got a call in the middle of the service from his girlfriend, Lauren Wagster.

Lauren just said, "It's Garrett - you need to come."

Tanya entered the home alone.

Brian and Garrett had an on-and-off volatile relationship so it was she who found their son in a crisis situation.

"I didn't recognize my own child's face," she said, her voice softening. He had gashes in his face, and he was just dirty. "Garrett was always a clean, prideful young man."

There were pill bottles on the floor, and when she opened a drawer to get something to wipe his face off she saw even more bottles.

Somehow, she got him into the vehicle and texted Brian.

They were at their breaking point and told Garrett he had to get help - he could choose where he was going, but he was going somewhere.

Tanya said she and Brian cried on the way to the rehab place. "It's hard to walk off and leave your child, but it was past our hands."

He would have to stay the first 30 days with no contact from his family. His birthday passed, then his dad's, and then Christmas. That was a hard month, Tanya acknowledged.

On about Day 28, however, the family surprised Garrett with a visit.

"He was a totally different man," she said.

His six months would be up in June, but in February her phone rang. "I picked it up and he said, 'Come get me.' And I did."

She went to Newport and picked him up at a park. Everything he owned was in a trash bag.

It wouldn't be long before he fell back in with the wrong crowd. "I told him you can't keep banging your head against the same wall and expect something different."

Garrett this time went to stay with Tanya's sister. "We knew he was in trouble."

It was March 15 when Tanya would get another urge to call Garrett. "God speaks to you and you can choose to ignore him or listen," she said.

That same night, Lauren had previously called the Yeagers to tell them her dog had been run over. About 10:30 that night, Brian was digging a grave for the dog and "in my mind, in my heart, I'm hearing, 'Call Garrett. Call Garrett."

But it was late and she talked herself out of making that call.

That decision would come back to haunt Tanya. She got up the next morning and went to work. Her phone rang at 8.

"The words I heard, the only thing she said to me was 'He's cold,' and I knew my boy was gone."

Tanya, who worked for Vital Link, said her co-workers had to tell her Garrett was dead. "When you have to hold your child, your grown child, the worst fear is what we are living - meaning one choice, in one night, completely changed our lives forever."

Garrett would leave behind his only child, Londyn Elizabeth, born November 14th, 2014.

I may not have been able to do anything. People make their own decisions and Garrett had his demons he struggled with during his life. But the fact that I did not speak up or follow up with Garrett after his time was done on our football team is not a mistake I will make

again. If you are working with young people, be sure to never leave things "unsaid" or turn a blind eye. Love them enough that you will call them out and work with them as much as you can.

This is a picture of Garrett his senior season. He is #41, a number that will not be worn at our school as long as

I am the coach. We invite Garrett's parents to come speak with our team every few years so that they can tell the football team about how small mistakes can lead to big ones that you can never take back. They bring his little daughter with them. As a coach, there may not have been anything I could have done to change the story, but from here on out it will not be due to lack of trying.

Recap

"If anyone, then, knows the good they ought to do and doesn't do it, it is sin for them." James 4:17

Discussion Questions
1. What mistakes have you made as a coach? Are you working to fix (if possible) those mistakes or learn from them?

2. Have you lost a player? How did it change your perception if you did?

Application
1. Reach out to an athlete on your team you worry may be heading down the wrong path. Share Garrett's story. Pray for that athlete and let them know you are praying for them to do what is right.

Ignoring The Noise

As a coach you will face what I often refer to as "the noise": Those in the stands or sometimes even in your own school building that may wish harm toward you or a player on your team. This is unfortunately a very common phenomenon in our profession. When "the noise" comes, and sometimes that noise sounds like a deafening roar, you must have a place you can go to gain strength. I hope that place is the scripture.

*11 The LORD said, "Go out and stand on the mountain in the presence of the LORD, for the LORD is about to pass by." Then a great and powerful wind tore the mountains apart and shattered the rocks before the LORD, but the LORD was not in the wind. After the wind there was an earthquake, but the LORD was not in the earthquake. 12 After the earthquake came a fire, but the LORD was not in the fire. And after the fire came a gentle whisper."*1 Kings 19:11-12

These verses come from the story of Elijah, but I feel they can apply to us today as coaches. Elijah had been feeling attacked on every side and was angry. He heard "the noise" from all around him and wanted God to be angry with him. When God told Elijah to wait, Elijah was

expecting retribution, but that is not often what happens. God needs us to be still and listen carefully to His wisdom. His wisdom can come in many forms. It can be a wise mentor, or a family member, or simply words from a minister. God will not abandon you, but as a coach we often don't listen to his encouragement.

The other "noise" I am referring to can be the praise from the outside. This can be worse than the criticism. People will honor you when times are good. It can become difficult to keep your focus where it belongs when you are being told how great you are. Just remember that clapping is not always directed at anything that will last. Those claps can turn to boos very quickly. If you are in the business for the awards and cheers, you may want to consider another career option.

They say "winning cures all"... until it doesn't. From a guy who has been "Coach of the Year" to 0-10, I can promise you "the noise" takes many forms and it will tear you apart if you let it. Be steadfast in your faith and realize that when your priorities don't rest on a scoreboard you are winning every day you mold your athletes.

I'll leave you with these words of encouragement:

"Blessed is the one who perseveres under trial because, having stood the test, that person will receive the crown of life that the Lord has promised to those who love him." James 1:12

About the Author

Coach Simpson is currently the Head Football Coach at Southside High School, a 4A school in Arkansas. Taking over a program that had won eight games in five seasons and had been on a 20+ game losing streak, Simpson has led Southside to the playoffs for four-consecutive seasons and won two conference titles in the past three seasons. For his efforts, he was named *4A-2 Conference Coach of the Year* (2017), named as a finalist for *Hooten's Coach of the Year* (2017), and has been the Arkansas All-Star Game Nominee for the 4A-2 (2016 and 2019).

This is Coach Simpson's 2nd book as he was a best-selling author for his first work: *Find a Way: What I wish I'd known when I became a Head Football Coach*. The book was released in 2019 and is available on Amazon. https://www.amazon.com/dp/1701924188

Simpson also serves as a Deacon of Education for the Highway church of Christ. He and his wife lead a coaches and families cruise clinic each year. For more information on his upcoming clinics contact FBCoachSimpson@gmail.com.

Simpson has also raised over $1.5 million for Southside and has overseen several major facility projects including: New Field Turf, Expansion to Fieldhouse, Expansion to the school's home bleachers, and the addition of a press box and a new video-board.

Prior to coming to Southside, Simpson took over as Head Coach at Alabama Christian Academy in Montgomery, Alabama. During his tenure there, Simpson took over a team that had been 4-18 and led them to their first home playoff game in over 20-years. For his efforts he was named Montgomery Advertiser's All-Metro Coach of the Year as well as being voted 4A Region 2 Coach of the Year (2010). Simpson also served as the head track coach at ACA and led the girls' and boys' teams to multiple top 10 finishes in 4A.

Simpson began his coaching career at Madison Academy, in Huntsville, Alabama. He served as a junior high basketball and football coach, before working into a varsity coaching role in football. He graduated from Harding University in 2003. He is married to Jamey and has three children: Avery, Braden and Bennett. The couple was married in 2001 after meeting at Harding University.

Made in the USA
Monee, IL
12 June 2020